MAKE ME LAUGH!

DON'T KID YOURSELF

Relatively Great (Family) Jokes

by Sam Schultz
pictures by Brian Gable

Carolrhoda Books, Inc. • Minneapolis

Mary: We've got a new baby at our house.

Terry: Is he going to stay?

Mary: I guess so. He brought all his clothes.

Willie: Dad, can I have $5 so I can go see Joey next door?

Dad: Why do you need $5 to go to see Joey?

Willie: Because his mother said he was at the movies!

Father: Why did you put that frog in your brother's bed?

Ellie: Because I couldn't find any worms!

Alfie: Dad, there's a small PTA meeting tomorrow that you have to come to.

Dad: If it's a small one, do I have to go?

Alfie: Yes, you have to go. It's just you, me, and my teacher.

Johnny: Will you marry me?

Jenny: You have to ask my father first.

Johnny: (later) Well, I asked him.

Jenny: And what did he say?

Johnny: He said he's already married.

Ann: Do you have a grandfather?

Jan: No, but he's okay.

Mother: Didn't I ask you to pick up your toys?

Son: I did, Mom—and when I was done playing, I put them down again!

Mother: Chuck, be careful with that hammer. You might hit your fingers.

Chuck: No I won't, Mom. Johnny's going to hold the nails.

Mother: Debby, I thought I told you to put salt in the saltshaker.

Debby: I tried, Mom, but I couldn't get the salt through those little holes!

Father: Emily, have you seen the newspaper?

Emily: Yes, Mother wrapped the garbage in it and threw it out.

Father: Darn. I'd like to have seen what was in it before she threw it out.

Emily: I can tell you what was in it, Daddy. Some chicken bones, coffee grounds, and old vegetables!

Timmy: My brother just got a puppy.

Jimmy: Do you help take care of him?

Timmy: No, my brother's old enough to take care of himself.

Father: Son, I've got a surprise for you. You've got a new baby sister!

Son: Oh! Does Mommy know about the surprise yet?

Q: What do you call your mother's father when he's good to you?

A: A Grand-father.

Teddy: Dad, can I please have a dime?

Dad: I think it's time you stopped asking me for dimes.

Teddy: Okay, how about a dollar?

Q: What always stays hot in the refrigerator?

A: Horseradish.

Voice over Phone: Is your mother home?

Girl: Yes, she is.

Voice: Will you call her to the phone, please?

Girl: Okay, but I'll have to go down the street to get her.

Voice: I thought you said she was home!

Girl: She is. This is my friend's house. I live down the street!

Mother: Jackie! It's after dark. You should have been home an hour ago.

Jackie: Why? What happened?

Ann: Our house is going to be warm this winter.

Pam: How do you know?

Ann: My father just painted it and he gave it two coats.

Q: What's a good time to go to the dentist?

A: Tooth-hurty (2:30).

Visitor: Can you play on the piano, Judy?

Judy: No, my mother won't let me climb up there.

Don: My father's a sound sleeper.

Ron: How do you know?

Don: His snoring wakes me up.

Dick: My father takes off his baseball cap to only one person.

Rick: Who's that?

Dick: His barber.

Susie: May I try on that dress in the window?

Salesperson: I'm sorry, ma'am, you'll have to do it in the dressing room!

Shawn: Does your mother tuck you in every night?

Darrin: No, she plugs me in. I have an electric blanket!

Mother: Bobby, there were 16 cookies in the cookie jar. Now there are only two. How do you explain that?

Bobby: I don't know, Mom. I thought I had gotten them all!

Mother: Would you like me to give you something for your cold?

Child: Yeah, how about a quarter?

Mother: How many times have I told you not to come home late for dinner?

Child: I didn't know I was supposed to keep score.

Q: Why was the boy called Sonny?

A: Because he was so bright.

Mark: My mother can make people do anything she wants them to.

Maya: Really? How does she do it?

Mark: She's a hypnotist!

Q: What should you take off before going to bed?

A: Your feet from the floor.

Mother: Your cough sounds much better this morning, Bridget.

Bridget: It should. I've been practicing all night!

Mother: Here, Peter, this dust brush will do half your work for you.

Peter: Great! Give me two of them.

Lauren: I have to go to the store to buy my mother some toothpaste.

Warren: Why, are her teeth loose?

First Boy: My brother won't give me anything of his.

Second Boy: Neither will mine. The only thing he ever gave me was chicken pox!

Mother: Tony, why is your little brother crying?

Tony: Because I won't give him any of my candy.

Mother: But I gave both of you candy. Has his been eaten already?

Tony: Yes, and he cried the whole time I was eating it.

Mother: Danielle! I told you to watch when the soup boils!

Danielle: I did, Mother. It boiled at exactly 6:15!

Mother: Why did you take the hot dogs out of the freezer?

Daughter: I was afraid they were too cold!

Mother: Wendy, please come into the kitchen and help me fix dinner.

Wendy: Why, is it broken?

Mother: Henry! How did the baby get all these bumps on his head?

Henry: Well, you said he was a bouncing baby boy. But I couldn't get him to bounce!

There was a young lad who said, "Why can't I have one more piece of pie?"
His mom said, "Pet,
you ate all you'll get."
So the lad could do nothing but cry.

Mother: Eat your green beans, Susie.
They'll put color in your cheeks.

Susie: Who wants green cheeks?

Johnny: My father bought my mother a new spring outfit.

Tammy: Really? What did he buy her?

Johnny: A rake, fertilizer, and some vegetable seeds.

Kendra: Mommy, Daddy just fell off the 25-foot ladder!

Mother: Oh, no! Is he hurt?

Kendra: No, he just fell off the first step.

Q: Why did Billy take a ruler to bed with him?

A: To see how long he slept!

Son: Dad, why are you spanking me? I admitted I chopped down the cherry tree. Even George Washington's father didn't spank him for that.

Father: Yes, but his father wasn't in the tree when it happened!

Uncle: Ally, I hear you went to the dentist today. Were you brave?

Ally: Yes!

Uncle: Well, for being brave, here's a dollar. Now tell me, what did the dentist do?

Ally: He pulled out one of my brother's teeth!

Mother: Jimmy, I thought I asked you to tell Billy that he could come here after supper.

Jimmy: That's what he's here after, Mom.

Dad: If you study hard, son, you'll get ahead.

Son: But Dad, I already have a head.

Sandy: Mom, is Dad still a growing boy?

Mom: No, why do you ask?

Sandy: Because his head is growing up through his hair.

Q: What kind of parent allows the kids to go to bed with their shoes on?

A: A horse.

Jimmy: What have you got in that bag?

Timmy: Oats. It's a birthday present for my uncle.

Jimmy: Why oats?

Timmy: Because my mother says he eats like a horse!

Jill: My pop can hold up a car with one hand.

Bill: Is he a weight lifter?

Jill: No, he's a traffic cop!

Jack: What makes you think your mother's trying to get rid of you?

Mack: Because she wraps my school lunch in a road map.

Young Man: I've come to ask for your daughter's hand in marriage.

Girl's Father: You've got to take all of her or it's no deal.

Betty: My sister caught her boyfriend flirting.

Jenny: That's how my sister caught her boyfriend, too.

Mother: My goodness, Jerry, who gave you that black eye?

Jerry: No one gave it to me. I had to fight for it!

Mother: Alice, tomorrow we're going to the doctor to have your eyes checked.

Alice: But Mom, you know I like polka dots better than checks!

Mike: I think my grandma must be a gardener.

Bobby: How come?

Mike: She says I grow like a weed.

Annie: Mother, the piano tuner is here.

Mother: Who sent for the piano tuner?

Annie: The neighbors!

Ike: I beat my brother up every morning.

Mike: Really?

Ike: Yep, I get up at seven, and he gets up at eight.

Phil: My dad shaves at least a dozen times a day.

Ronnie: How come?

Phil: He's a barber.

Charlie: What are you giving your mom and dad for Christmas?

Artie: A list of everything I want.

Q: What's the best way to make anti-freeze?

A: Take away her electric blanket!

Mother: Charles, why are you standing in front of that mirror with your eyes closed?

Charles: I want to see what I look like when I'm asleep!

Danny: My father's studying to be an astronaut.

Manny: That a fact?

Danny: Yep. His boss called my mother and told her Pop was taking up space!

Ellen: Our scout troup is going on a 10-mile hike!

Dad: When I was your age, I thought nothing of walking 10 miles.

Ellen: I don't think much of it, either.

Aunt: Would you like to teach your new baby brother how to talk, Susie?

Susie: No, I'd like to teach him how to be quiet.

Mother: Billy, why is it that you get into more trouble than anyone else in the family?

Billy: I guess it's because I get up first.

Mae: My baby brother was born in a hospital.

Fay: Why? Was he sick?

Mother: Georgie, will you please take this pot of soup across the street to the Smiths, and find out how old Mrs. Smith is?

Georgie: (Returning) Mrs. Smith said it's none of your business how old she is!

Mother: Junior, why did you put mud in your sister's mouth?

Junior: Because it was open!

Q: Why did Junior put ice in his father's bed?

A: Because he wanted a cold pop.

Julie: I'm writing a letter to my dog Fido.

Jill: But you don't know how to write.

Julie: That's okay. Fido doesn't know how to read!

Mom: It's going to hurt me to punish you, Son.

Son: Then don't do it, Mom. I don't want you to hurt yourself.

Mother: How did you get that hole in your new pants?

Jeff: I fell off the swings.

Mother: Why did you do that in your new pants?

Jeff: I didn't have time to take them off!

Jason: Where did you get those beautiful eyes?

Jessica: Oh, they came with my face.

Q: What do you call a dead parrot?

A: A polygone.

Marty: Mom, baby sister just swallowed my pencil.

Mom: My goodness, we've got to do something about that.

Marty: No, it's okay, Mom. I've got other pencils.

Father: Patty, would you like to join me in a bowl of soup?

Patty: Do you think there'd be room for the two of us?

Dylan: Why are you looking so sad?

Ryan: We're supposed to go on vacation tomorrow, but my mother always gets sick the night before we leave.

Dylan: Then why don't you leave a day early?

There once was a girl named Flack,
Who lost her best dolly named Jack.
"Don't cry," said her mother,
"I'll buy you another."
Said Flack, "No. I just want Jack back!"

Q: What would you call your brother if he was afraid to swim in the ocean?

A: Chicken of the Sea.

Mary: My father's a light sleeper.

Harry: Not my father. He sleeps in the dark.

Molly: My mother cooked for 100 people yesterday.

Polly: What was the occasion?

Molly: No occasion. She works in a restaurant.

Susie: I always have to help my little brother catch the bus.

Matt: How come?

Susie: He's not strong enough to catch a bus by himself!

Ned: My brother sleeps on the bedroom chandelier.

Fred: Why?

Ned: Because he's a light sleeper!

Bess: My brother has three feet.

Tess: How do you know?

Bess: He wrote my mother from college that he grew another foot.

Danny: Mother! The dog next door just bit off my toe.

Mother: You can't come in the house now, Danny. I just washed the floor.

Mother: Denny, how did you get your pants so wet?

Denny: I just washed them.

Mother: But why don't you let them dry before you put them on?

Denny: Because the label says, "Wash and Wear!"

Salesman: Will these stairs take me up to your house?

Little Boy: No, you have to climb them.

Tillie: (At restaurant) Mom, I can't eat this hamburger. It tastes awful!

Mother: Do you want me to call the waiter?

Tillie: No, I don't think he'll be able to eat it, either.

Father: Son, when you grow up I want you to be a gentleman.

Son: But I don't want to be a gentleman. I want to be just like you!

Delivery Man: Young man, is your mother home?

Young Man: Do you think I'd be pulling these weeds if she wasn't?

Q: Why are baby girls dressed in pink and baby boys dressed in blue?

A: Because they can't dress themselves.

Mother: Mickey, I can't hear you saying your prayers.

Mickey: That's because I'm not talking to you.

Mother: You can't leave this house until you finish your alphabet soup.

Daughter: Honest, Mom, I can't eat another word.

Mother: Joey, why did I catch you with your hand in the cookie jar?

Joey: Because I didn't hear you coming!

Ellie: When my mother's down in the dumps she always gets a new dress.

Nellie: I thought that's where she got them.

Q: Why did the little boy's mother make him go to his bed?

A: Because the bed couldn't come to him!

This book is available in two editions:
Library binding by Carolrhoda Books, Inc.,
  a division of Lerner Publishing Group
Soft cover by First Avenue Editions,
  an imprint of Lerner Publishing Group
241 First Avenue North
Minneapolis, MN 55401 U.S.A.

Website address: www.lernerbooks.com

Library of Congress Cataloging-in-Publication Data

Schultz, Sam.
    Don't kid yourself : relatively great (family) jokes / by Sam Schultz ; illustrations
by Brian Gable.
      p.   cm. — (Make me laugh)
    ISBN: 1–57505–641–0 (lib. bdg. : alk. paper)
    ISBN: 1–57505–701–8 (pbk. : alk. paper)
    1. Wit and humor, Juvenile. I. Gable, Brian, 1949– II. Title. III. Series.
PN6166.S38 2004
818'.5402—dc21   2002015788

Manufactured in the United States of America
1 2 3 4 5 6 – JR – 09 08 07 06 05 04